How Many
How Many
How Many

For Ann —
Let me count the ways.

R. W.

For my parents

C. J.

Text copyright © 1993 by Rick Walton
Illustrations copyright © 1993 by Cynthia Jabar

First U.S. paperback edition 1996

The Library of Congress has cataloged the hardcover edition as follows:

Walton, Rick.
How many, how many, how many / written by Rick Walton ;
illustrated by Cynthia Jabar.
Summary: The reader counts from one to twelve while guessing the answers
to questions about nursery rhymes, names of the seasons, players
on a football team, and other basic information.
ISBN 978-1-56402-062-8 (hardcover)
1. Counting — Juvenile literature. [1. Counting. 2. Questions and answers.]
I. Jabar, Cynthia, ill. II. Title
QA113.W35   1993
513.2'11 — dc20
[E]   92-54408

ISBN 978-1-56402-656-9 (paperback)

16 SWT 23 22 21 20 19 18 17 16

Printed in Dongguan, Guangdong, China

This book was typeset in New Baskerville.
The illustrations were done on scratchboard.

Candlewick Press
99 Dover Street
Somerville, Massachusetts 02144

visit us at www.candlewick.com

How Many
How Many
How Many

Rick Walton   illustrated by Cynthia Jabar

CANDLEWICK PRESS

Are you ready? Tell me yes.
How many HOW MANYs can you guess?

Count them, name them, ready, go!
How many HOW MANYs do you know?

He is nimble. He is quick.
How many jump the candlestick?

= 1

One

Jack.

Spiders like to steal her seat.
How many things does Muffet eat?

Two
Curds and whey.

Here Goldilocks sleeps all alone.
How many bears are coming home?

Three
The mama bear, the papa bear, and the baby bear.

Snowy, cloudy, sunny, clear.
How many seasons in a year?

Four
Winter, spring,
summer, fall.

Pearl ring, gold ring, wedding band.
How many fingers on your hand?

Five

Little finger, ring finger, middle finger,
index finger, thumb.

See them hunting on the lawn.
How many legs do ants walk on?

Six

Left fore, right fore, left middle,
right middle, left hind, right hind.

Rainbows follow storms in March.
How many colors in the arch?

Seven

Red, orange, yellow, green, blue, indigo, violet.

Santa flies up, up away!
How many reindeer pull his sleigh?

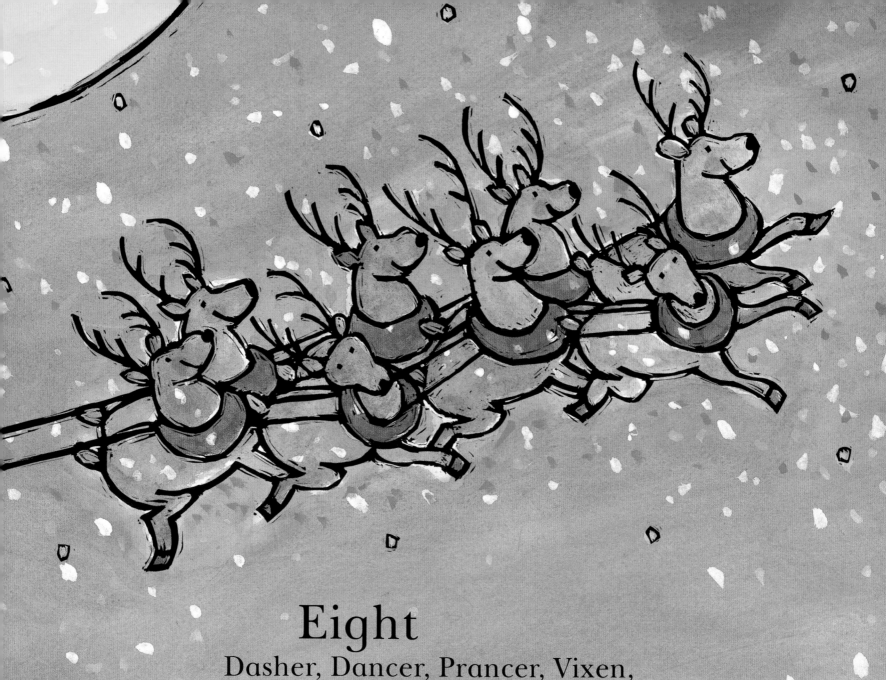

Eight
Dasher, Dancer, Prancer, Vixen,
Comet, Cupid, Donner, Blitzen.

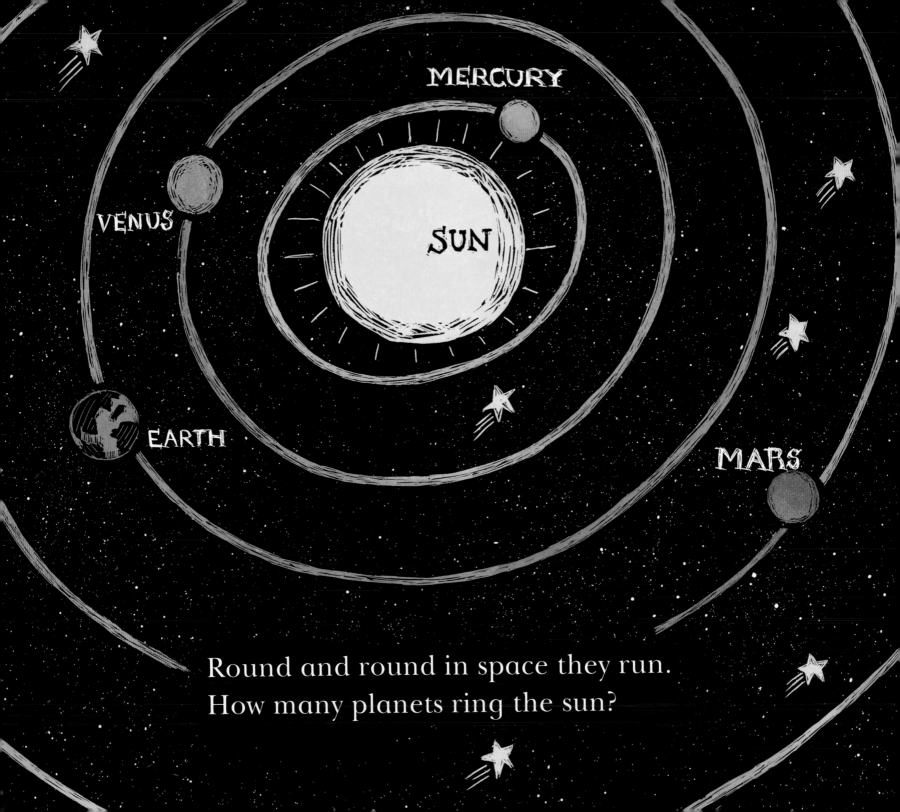

MERCURY

VENUS

SUN

EARTH

MARS

Round and round in space they run.
How many planets ring the sun?

Nine
Mercury, Venus, Earth,
Mars, Jupiter, Saturn,
Uranus, Neptune, Pluto.

Call me if you feel alone.
How many numbers on a phone?

Ten

Zero, one, two, three, four, five,
six, seven, eight, nine.

It's a goal! The players scream.
How many on a soccer team?

fullback

right midfielder

right winger

Striker

stopper

goalkeeper

sweeper

fullback

center

Eleven

Left winger, left midfielder,
fullback, fullback, stopper, sweeper,
right winger, right midfielder,
striker, center, goalkeeper.

left winger

left midfielder

Holidays are almost here.
How many months make up a year?

Twelve

January, February, March, April, May, June, July,
August, September, October, November, December.

Were you counting? Tell me yes.
How many HOW MANYs did you guess?

And were you looking carefully?
Somewhere did you also see . . .